KATSURA OTOKO

Ninjutsu Training for the Lone Practitioner

Katsura Otoko

The *Lone Shinobi* operates wthout support, as if he were the *Man on the Moon*

KATSURA OTOKO

Ninjutsu Training for the Lone Practitioner

桂男

JAMES LORIEGA

LOST ARTS
PUBLICATIONS

First Printing: November 2018

ISBN: 978-0-359-25288-6

Lost Arts Publications
Brooklyn, NY 11235

LOST ARTS
PUBLICATIONS

Dedication

Disclaimer Notice

KATSURA OTOKO

Ninjutsu Training for the Lone Practitioner

Contents

The concept of *Katsura Otoko* from an old Japanese print

PREFACE

There was once a time was when ninjutsu training was scarce, and when that very scarcity inspired its few and fortunate practitioners to be diligent and motivated. Back then, if you were privileged enough to have access to legitimate training, you practiced earnestly and untiringly in order to benefit from that rare opportunity.

That is not the case today, when that once-scarce *Taijutsu* training has become as ubiquitous as *Tai Chi* or *Tae Bo*. But that, too, can be as much a problem as a blessing because—as with everything else—market saturation often brings with it a mediocrity of product or service. Witness the "McDojo phenomenon" of recent decades and you can see the dilution of *karate, taekwondo,* and *Brazilian jujutsu* schools into training venues that operate primarily for the purposes of baby-sitting, ego aggrandizement, and dollar generation for their dojo operators (*operators*, being the functional word.)

There are, to be certain, veteran *shinobi* practitioners who feel that contemporary Ninjutsu training is following—or has *already* followed —the *Way of McDojos*. Traditional martial ideals and standards seem to be compromised, disregarded, and at times even perverted. The venerable Bujinkan has in many instances become the *Bujin con*, with their supposed Iga-ryu Ninjutsu taught by instructors pandering to students who are far more interested in the inflated belt rankings of Ego-ryu. Yet that is but a minor flaw.

Ninjutsu is Intelligence-Gathering

Its primary objective is to uncover information and report it to one's clan, leader, or employer.

To accomplish this, the ninja relies on a broad variety of physical skills and psychological strategies.

Taijutsu is But One of Aspect of Ninjutsu

The skills of stealth, infiltration, observation, accurate assessment, deception, and not being discovered are the ninja's paramount concern, and represent his priority and focus of training.

Acquiring these primary skills requires formal training time. Without them, the practitioner is merely a skilled jujutsu-ka, not a shinobi-ka or ninja

No Skills in Intelligence-Gathering:
No Stealth, Infiltration, Observation, Accurate Assessment, Deception, or Not Being Discovered, etc...
Where is the Ninjutsu?

Taijutsu is Not Ninjutsu

As depicted by the illustation on the left, many modern practitioners dedicate the bulk of their training engaged in combat arts (armed and unarmed) and spend little if any time on the more relevant shinobi arts

Since the time of the "Second Ninja Boom" of the 1980s, the "ninja experts" have led novices to believe by that Taijutsu *is* Ninjutsu. Highly-ranked instructors, who one assumes would know otherwise, have also perpetuated this erroneous notion among their student followers. (While I have my own theory of why they do this, that speculation be addressed in a subsequent work.)

Martial arts publications are equally complicit in perpetuating this false notion because *unarmed combat*, and not how to effectively avoid it, is what sells their magazines. The actual elements of Ninjutsu— intelligence-gathering, strategy, invisibility, etc.—seem to all fall inconveniently outside of their of their *block-punch-kick-and-throw* paradigm. As Technical Editor for NINJA magazine for ten years, I can say that presenting the truer aspects of the art could be often difficult.

The intended purpose of this book is to provide, in some basic measure, a more authentic and balanced understanding of what traditional ninjutsu was—and of what it can still be.

This book is intended for those practitioners, once affiliated with a ninjutsu system or dojo, who may have become disillusioned with the quality or authenticity of training. They believe in and espouse ninjutsu's tenets but have lost their faith in their leadership. They want to continue following **Shinobi-no-Michi**, the *Path of Ninjutsu*, but who don't necessarily feel the need to follow another person's interpretation, or misinterpretation, of it.

This book is also intended for readers without a dojo affiliation who are nonetheless interested in practicing ninjutsu. For them, this work was to provide my *new* students with a bird's-eye view of what ninjutsu encompasses. For them, this excerpt functions as a *shorthand* reminder that their training focus must remain *broad-based* and *multi-faceted*.

And, finally, this book will equally serve as a tangible asset to active ninjutsu practitioners, regardless of dojo or political[1] affiliation, who *are* content and satisfied with the current quality of their instruction. It will seamlessly complement their training and provide them with an ancillary curriculum to broaden their skills. It will, for all readers, function as a portable ninjutsu dojo when they are away from formal training, whether they are off on a vacation in the South of France or a tour of duty in Northern Afghanistan.

---

1 Political in the sense of ninjutsu styles.

Part I:

The Philosophical Components

桂男

THE CORE OF NINJUTSU

All ninjutsu begins and ends with philosophy, and this is as much the case when living as a solitary ninja as when practicing any other aspect of *shinobijutsu*. Philosophical principles comprise the core of the ninja's belief system and provide him with the solace he needs to remain constant and consistent in his actions and his thinking.

This book will not cover *taijutsu* tactics or *unarmed fighting* techniques as these are typically the mainstay of "ninjutsu" dojo around the globe. (And in any case, *taijutsu*, if anything, is synonymous with *jujutsu*, not ninjutsu.) While I have been pleasantly surprised, two or three times, in finding dojo that actually teach a full spectrum of ninjutsu arts—not *unarmed fighting* arts—these have been not only few but, sadly, the rare exception.

In fact, I have actually witnessed ninjutsu training in dojo that don't purport to teach ninjutsu at all. Those dojo, not surprisingly when you stop to think about it, are dedicated to instruction in the samurai disciplines. Such schools adhere to very traditional curricula, encompassing the unarmed fighting arts, the arts of using the sword (per the established dictates of some formal *kenjutsu ryu*, not made-up *kata* and *waza* "developed" in some "ninja sensei's" backyard), varied auxiliary arts (*hojojtsu, juttejutsu, shurikenjutsu,* etc.), the principles of *Bukyo*, and the study of *Heiho*.

The Concept of *Katsura Otoko*

The premise for this book derives from the concept of **katsura otoko**, one of ten traditional ninjutsu infiltration tactics, used when operating behind enemy lines. Collectively, the tactics were known as *Toiri-no-jutsu*, and of these the tactic of *katsura otoko* proposes that the secret agent residing and working inside enemy territory must be prepared to *operate alone and independently for as long as it takes* to accomplish his or her mission. Historically, such assignments required the ninja to function as an agent-in-place and serve for months, or even years, without the benefit of assistance or support from fellow *shinobi* or other members of his clan. To that point, the term *katsura otoko* implied that the lone ninja was as solitary and isolated as the *man on the moon*[2].

We find in the notion of *katsura otoko* an apt metaphor for the types of readers referenced earlier:

- *the person interested in practicing ninjutsu but lacking affiliation wth a dojo;*
- *the practitioner who is affiliated with a ninjutsu system but who is disillusioned with the quality or authenticity of training; and*
- *the practitioner who is active and progressing in ninjutsu and is concurrently seeking to further expand or augment his knowledge and understanding.*

Whichever category you find yourself in, approach the information in this book as if you are a lone ninja, emplaced behind enemy lines, and

---

2 The literal meaning of *katsura otoko*.

striving merely to remain safe, sane, secure, and anonymous—a lone ninja who fully understands that maintaining self-sufficiency and safeguarding one's autonomy requires proactive vigilance a well as routine diligence.

A Word on Word Use

Through over-use and abuse, the terms *ninja* and *ninjutsu* have reached the point of being meaningless, as much in the practice of the martial arts as in our culture. In our culture, the term *ninja* is liberally used when referring to everything from cartoon turtles to motorcycles to food processors.

In the martial arts, we now hear the term *ninja* used in connecction with after-school babysitting classes that take place in local dojo. However, unless the young children in those ubiquitous "Ninja After-School Programs" are actually leaning to spy, steal, and discover the secrets of their "enemies," the use of the term *ninja* is as insignificant as it is erroneous.

The same can be said of the term *ninjutsu*, an art which many claim to teach but very few actually do. The majority of instructors who focus almost exclusively on taijutsu cannot be regarded as teaching ninjutsu. More to the point, the individual who is truly skilled in ninjutsu will have little occasion to need, let alone *use*, taijutsu. To dissociate from popular culture adopters who use the terms casually, and from martial arts practitioners who use the terms fraudulently—and ignorantly—

we will instead utilize the terms *shinobi* and *traditional ninjutsu* throughout this book.

Background on Toiri-no-jutsu

In 1959, the reknown ninjutsu researcher **Heishichiro Okuse** authored a book titled, **Ninjutsu Hiden 忍術秘伝**, or *Secret Writings of Ninjutsu*. From the early 70s until the time of his passing, Heishichiro Okuse was cited as being "The foremost authority on Ninjitsu [sic] in Japan." Among the vast technical information contained in his **Ninjutsu Hiden** was a section on *Toiri-no-jutsu*.

As Okuse explained it, shinobi were potenially trained in ten discrete *Toiri-no-jutsu* tactics that were used in laying the groundwork prior to the outbreak of battle. The first of these tactics was called *katsura otoko-no-jutsu*, or *the method of the Man on the Moon*. Okuse explained that a shinobi operating in enemy territory was called *katsura otoko* because he was almost as isolated as if he were living on the moon. In all, the ten *toiri-no-jutsu* were as follows[3]:

1. Katsura otoko-no-jutsu
2. Joei-no-jutsu
3. Kunoichi-no-jutsu
4. Satobito-no-jutsu
5. Minomushi-no-jutsu
6. Hotarubi-no-jutsu
7. Fukuro-gaeshi-no-jutsu
8. Tensui-no-jutsu
9. Chikyu-no-jutsu
10. Yamabiko-no-jutsu

---

3 A fuller explanation of the ten *toiri* tactics can be found in Andrew Adams' classic book, **Ninja: The Invisible Assassins**

WHAT IS NINJUTSU

In 1938, Fujita Seiko published a collection of his lectures under the title, **What is Ninjutsu?**[4] Fujita, of course, was the 14th Headmaster of the Wada lineage of Kōuga-ryu Ninjutsu, and regarded by most knowledgeable shinobi practitioners to have been the *last true ninja*. While others make claim to this honorific, none were officially operational in actual wartime activities as was Fujita, both before and during World War II. The question posed by the title of Fujita's book, one of many he wrote, is still asked by novices today.

Casual leafing through the pages of most martial arts book catalogs will reveal whole sections dedicated to primers, manuals, and texts on the various discrete shinobi arts, as well as to tomes on ninjutsu in general. It might seem incredible to us now that there was ever a time when the slightest information on ninjutsu and the shinobi was scarce. Inevitably, when you read the bulk of books on the subject you get a variety of definitions, many of them contradictory to one another. Nonetheless, the fact remains that what little information did exist on these now-familiar subjects thirty years ago was hard to find and, when found, often hard to understand.

The very first technical information on ninjutsu to appear in the United States in English is a true treasure for various reasons. First, because it gave those American readers lucky enough to stumble

4 Available in a English-Japanese translation by Eric Shahan.

across it an initial *unbiased* glimpse of this now well-known art; second, because its author provided objective insights the likes of which are rare today; and third, because his explanations of the shinobi arts were refreshingly more practical than much of the pseudo-spiritual nonsensical rhetoric that passes for ninjutsu gospel today. Below is an excerpt from this first appearance of the ninja in the U.S.:

> *Here is the main lesson to be learned from the ninja—his walk ... The ninja never swaggered ... His walk is light, straight and swift, yet unhurried. This is the secret of remaining unobtrusive, of 'disappearing' by remaining unnoticed. A master of this walk finds it easy to become a human chameleon, to blend with the motion around him, or the motionlessness. He will walk into a group of teenagers and saunter along with them, into a group of old folks and adjust his pace to their faltering steps, or he can walk down a quiet street, alone, and never be noticed. People may look at him, but they will not see him. The main magic of the ninja was and is the magic of his walk.*

The year was 1962. The writer was Jay Gluck, and the book, **Zen Combat**. Since then, scores of books have been written in English on the physical and mystical aspects of ninjutsu and the lofty attributes of the ninja. Surprisingly however, not one book has been published on the basic subject of his walk. (We should perhaps regard the fact that nothing has been published on the fundamental subject of walking as still another of the many mysteries surrounding ninjutsu!)

20

Traditional ninjutsu evolved over many centuries, adopting many cultural, military, and psychological influences, from many and diverse sources. It was developed by an untold number of families, clans, and military groups, each with its own perspectives, motives, and specializations. This is why one can find almost as many definitions of the term ninjutsu as there are books on the subject. This is also why the best way to understand ninjutsu is to understand the purposes for which its methods were used, and not by becoming fixated on "the quality of your taijutsu."

Some traditional ninjutsu methods focused on espionage; others on disseminating misinformation and creating dissent; and some on military operations, such as sabotage and assassination. All of these purposes required an aptitude for stealth, secrecy, and invisibility which explains why ninjutsu was alternately referred to as the *art of stealth*, the *art of secrecy*, and the *art of invisibility*.

Such purposes—*stealth*, *secrecy*, and *invisibility*—also required that the shinobi possess great fortitude and forbearance. Thus, the root character *nin* which defines the art of *nin*jutsu and its practitioner, the *nin*ja, can be translated as constancy, persistence, and perseverance. Thus, ninjutsu is also referred to as the *art of endurance*.

Yet such interpretations described only the shinobi's *personal* attributes. To describe the shinobi's martial skills we need to understand the late Donn F. Draeger's interpretation of the art of ninjutsu: *the Art of Protecting Against Danger*. Draeger's insight into the art—an insight born of extensive academic research coupled with physical training—eloquently summarizes the detailed comprehensiveness of the shinobi's disciplines. Seen from that perspective, the over-emphasized concern with taijutsu becomes the mere, and relatively-insignificant, tip of the ninjutsu iceberg.

If you belong to an "authentic" ninjutsu organization, you may be incredulously asking, *Wait. Are you purporting that my Ninpo Taijutsu is not Ninjutsu?* In asking you have answered your own question. *So, what then is Ninjutsu?*

According to some of the popular sources, ninjutsu is an art first pioneered by, alternateLy, the monk *En-no-Gyoja*, or the warrior *Minamoto no Yoshitsune*[5], or the spy *Otomo-no-Saijin*, the first individual to be given the name "Shinobi" by Prince Regent Shotoku Taishi, sometime during the *Asuka* period (592-710). From there, the art is supposedly further developed and refined by, again alternately, Chinese expatriates living in Japan, or mountain-dwelling warrior monks called *yamabushi*, or disenfranchised samurai, or various others.

To truly understand the concept of ninjutsu, however, we need to go farther back into history, and far beyond the geographical borders of what later became Japan, where we can find the ninjutsu's original DNA. That time is the latter part of the Zhou Dynasty (722-481 BCE) and the place, the Kingdom of Wu, in China.

---

5 Half-brother of the first Kamakura shogun

DIVINE MANIPULATION OF THREADS

According to Japanese history, the military treatise known as **The Art of War** was introduced to Japan by Kibi-no-Makibi. He lived from 693 to 775 and resided in China for almost twenty years. Notations in the **Shoku Nihongi** (*Supplementary Annals of Japan*) indicate that Kibi-no-Makibi was instructing Japanese warriors in the precepts of the *Art of War* well before 760.

In the twelfth century, *Minamoto Yoshitsune* was reputedly an expert in applying the strategies of the *Sonshi-no-Heiho*, as the *Art of War* is called in Japanese. Another ancient Japanese record, the *Taiheiki* (*Chronicles of Pacification of the Realm*), documents the fact that samurai were made familiar with the teachings of the book, although relatively few copies were in existence. But how was the wisdom of the *Sonshi* disseminated? In **A History of Japan**, author James Murdoch tells us that,

> "... *at night a professor would be set to read* [Chinese manuals] *aloud to the samurai gathered in the castle wall to hear him ... What was chiefly expounded was not so much the principles of war as the dirtiest form of statecraft with its unspeakable depths of duplicity...*"

Murdoch also mentions that, specifically,

> "*Sonshi's section on spies is truly abominable and revolting; yet this special section on spies must be carefully conned by anyone who wished to understand the fashion in which war was waged in Japan at this time.*"

One translator of the *Sonshi*, Samuel B. Griffith, supports this, saying that feudal Japan's four famous warrior generals—*Oda Nobunaga*, *Toyotomi Hideyoshi*, *Tokugawa Ieyasu*, and *Takeda Shingen*—were all thoroughly versed in Chinese military classics. Historically-astute ninjutsu practitioners will also note that all four men were well known for having routinely employed shinobi in their military campaigns. Tokugawa Ieyasu, for example, outlawed the practice of ninutsu but actually retained the services of at least three separate shinobi factions – the *Ura-Yagyu*, the *Kouga*, and the *Iga*.

Takeda Shingen in particular was a master of deception who believed that *"...in his struggle for power ... assassination* [was] *a perfectly legitimate way to dispose of a rival."* In fact, he not only lived by the *Sonshi*'s precepts, but actually adopted the advice of its seventh chapter as his clan's motto:

> *"Swift as the Wind,*
> *Silent as a Forest,*
> *Fierce as Fire and*
> *Immovable as a Mountain[6]."*

The Divine Thread

As concerns ninjutsu, the most relevant of the *Thirteen Chapters*, as the *Sonshi* is also referred to, is the final one, which addresses the proper use of spies and secret agents. Titled *The Divine Thread* in some editions, this chapter informs the reader that,

> *"What enables the wise sovereign and the good general to strike and conquer, and achieve things beyond the reach of ordinary men, is foreknowledge.[7]"*

---

6 In Japanese, *Fūrin Kazan*.
7 That, after all, was what the ninja was trained for and hired to provide.

As Griffith explains it,

> "*Prior to hostilities, secret agents separated the enemy's subversive activities. Among their missions were to spread false rumors and misleading information, to corrupt and subvert officials, to create and exacerbate internal discord, and to nurture Fifth Columns. Meanwhile, spies active at all levels ascertained the enemy's position. On their reports, 'victorious plans' were based.*"

The Invisible Assassins

In **Ninja**: *The Invisible Assassins*, an early and somewhat sensationalized overview of ninjutsu, author Andrew Adams writes,

> "*Ninjutsu is supposed to have originated more that 2,000 years ago as a treatise on the art of spying in the ancient Chinese book on military science called Sun Tzu.*" He continues, "*It was written by the great Chinese strategist Sun [Tzu] Wu who lived between 500 and 300 B.C.*"

In truth, to this day we do not know if a person named "Sun Wu Tzu," or *Sonbu*, as the Japanese refer to him, actually existed. According to Griffith, there has always been great controversy and mystery surrounding the work's provenance. What *is* known is that while many people mistakenly believe that Sun Tzu means "The Art of War," this is actually the author's name. The correct Chinese title for the *Art of War* is actually *Ping Fa*, which can mean *The Art or War*, as well as *The Way of Strategy*.

The Codification of Ninjutsu

In a slim tome he titled **Ninjutsu: The Art of Invisibility**, the aforementioned arts practitioner and scholar, Donn F. Draeger, also refers to *Sonshi* as having been the reference source for the first

Japanese codification of ninjutsu. Like Adams, Draeger believed that it is conceivable that the roots of what would later be termed *ninjutsu* were brought to Japan from China. However, lest bandwagoning Chinese martial artists begin making claims to being the forerunners of *ninjutsu*, Draeger is quick to point out that, "*... like much else in Japanese culture which stems from foreign sources of influence, ninjutsu quickly became Japanized.*"

With regard to the treatise, Draeger states that, "*The* [Sonshi] *may have been brought to Japan as early as the sixth century A.D.*" He proceeds to explain that, "*By the time of the rise to power of the professional warrior class in the 12th century, all successful military commanders employed specialists in ninjutsu. They made the Sonshi their standard text.*" Below is the thirteenth chapter of the Sonshi, The Divine Thread.

In the Sonshi is written:

Raising an army of a hundred thousand and advancing it a thousand li, the expenses to the people and the nation's resources are one thousand gold pieces a day.

Those in commotion internally and externally, those exhausted on the roads, and those unable to do their daily work are seven hundred thousand families.

Two sides remain in standoff for several years in order to do battle for a decisive victory on a single day.

Yet one refusing to outlay a hundred pieces of gold and thereby does not know the enemy's situation is the height of inhumanity.

This one is not the general of the people, a help to the ruler, or the master of victory.

What enables the enlightened rulers and good generals to conquer the enemy at every move and achieve extraordinary success is foreknowledge.

Foreknowledge cannot be elicited from ghosts and spirits; It cannot be inferred from comparison of previous events, or from the calculations of the heavens, but must be obtained from people who have knowledge of the enemy's situation.

Therefore, five types of spies are used. In Ninjutsu, we call the five types Gokan:
> *Local spies,*
> *Internal spies,*
> *Turned spies,*
> *Exendable spies, and*
> *Living spies.*

*When all five are used, and no one knows their Way, it is called the **Divine Manipulation of the Threads,** and it is the ruler's treasure.*

*For local spies, we use the enemy's people. In Ninjutsu, we call such spies **Kyokan.***
*For internal spies we use the enemy's officials. We call these spies **Naikan.***
*For turned spies[8] we use the enemy's spies. We call these spies **Hankan.***
*For expendable spies we use agents to spread mis-information to the enemy. We call these **Shikan.***
*For living spies[9], we use agents to return with reports. We call these **Shokan.***

---

8 The first three types—*local, internal,* and *double*—are from the enemy's ranks and known as **turned spies**.
9 The last two types—alternately known as *dead* and *surviving* spies—are from the general's own ranks.

Therefore, of those close to the army, none is closer than spies, no reward more generously given, and no matter in greater secrecy.

Only the wisest ruler can use spies; only the most benevolent and upright general can use spies, and only the most alert and observant person can get the truth using spies. It is subtle, subtle!

There is nowhere that spies cannot be used.

If a spy's activities are leaked before they are to begin, the spy and those who know should be put to death.

If you want to attack an army, besiege a walled city, assassinate individuals, you must know the identities of the defending generals, assistants, associates, gate guards, and officers. You must have spies seek and learn them.

You must seek enemy spies. Bribe them, and instruct and retain them.

Therefore, turned spies can be obtained and used.
From their knowledge, you can obtain local and internal spies.

From their knowledge, the dead spies can spread misinformation to the enemy. From their knowledge, our living spies can be used as planned.

The ruler must know these five kinds of espionage.

This knowledge depends on the double spies. Therefore, you must treat them with the utmost generosity. In ancient times, the rise of the Yin dynasty was due to I Chih, who served the house of Hsia; the rise of the Chou dynasty was due to Lu Ya, who served the house of Yin. Therefore, enlightened rulers and good generals who are able to obtain intelligent agents as spies are certain for great achievements.

They are essential for warfare, and what the army depends on to be victorious.

Thus we see that, as stated at the outset of Chapter 1, *All ninjutsu begins and ends with philosophy.* Beyond this initial philosophical kernal, which dates back a few thousand years, there are other relevant and *relatively*-recent philosophical writings that can provide guidelines for aligning one's solitary path with the *Way of Ninjutsu.*

I have no enemy; I make a lack of caution my enemy

PHILOSOPHICAL GUIDELINES

The twenty-two Zen assertions known as **The Samurai Creed** were reputedly written in the 13th century. These dicta have been ascribed to the strategist, Yamamoto Kansuke, the spymaster for Takeda Shingen, as well as to the *kenshin*[10], Musashi Miyamoto. However, Kansuke died in 1561, and Musashi in 1646; thus, either the date is incorrect, or the creed was not authored by either Takeda's strategist or the swordsman from Musashi.

The earliest English-language translation of The Samurai Creed appears in E.J. Harrison's **The Fighting Spirit of Japan**, first published around 1912. The Creed became more widely-known in the late 1960s with the publication of Charles Gruzanski's, **Spike and Chain**, a very early book that focused on two lesser-known weapon arts of the bushi and shinobi. Since that time, the Creed has been oft-quoted (and often misinterpreted) by martial arts writers from all fighting disciplines. Yet, despite its uncertain provenance and its many imprecise "interpretations," the Creed represents an invaluable resource for aspiring and practicing ninjutsu practitioners seeking to align their training and their lives with an ausere but authentic *Path of the Warrior*, to use a trite expression. For the rare reader who has not yet seen it, The Samurai Creed follows in its most original form. Interpet it as you will ... you are a lone practitioner.

---

10 "Sword saint," and posthumous title awarded to Musashi.

The Samurai Creed

I have no parents; I make the heavens and the earth my parents.

*I have no home; I make **seika tanden**[11] (abdomenal region) my home.*

I have no divine power; I make honesty my divine power.

I have no means; I make docility my means.

I have no magic power; I make personality my magic power.

*I have neither life nor death; I make of **a um** (the art of regulating one's breath) my life and death.*

I have no body; I make stoicism my body.

I have no eyes; I make the flash of lightning my eyes.

I have no ears; I make sensibility my ears.

I have no limbs; I make promptitude my limbs.

I have no laws; I make self-protection my laws.

*I have no strategy; I make **sakkatsu jizai**[12] (free to kill and free to restore life) my strategy.*

*I have no designs; I make **kisan** (seizing opportunity by the forelock) my designs.*

I have no miracles; I make righteous laws my miracle.

*I have no principles; I make **rinkiohen** (adaptability to all circumstances) my principle.*

*I have no tactics; I make **kyo-jitsu** (emptiness and fullness) my tactics.*

*I have no talent; I make **toi sokumyo**[13] (ready wit) my talent.*

I have no friends; I make my mind my friend.

I have no enemies; I make a lack of caution my enemy.

*I have no armor; I make **jin-gi**[14] (benevolence and righteousness[15]) my armor.*

*I have no castle; I make **fudoshin** (immovable mind) my castle.*

*I have no sword; I make **mushin** (absence of self) my sword.*

---

11 Another term for the *hara*.

12 This is similar to the samurai privilege of *Kirisute Gomen*, the warrior's right to kill and walk away.

13 This is the attribute of *resourcefulness* that is so critical for spies and covert agents.

14 These virtues are taken directly from *Bushido*, the code of conduct of the Bushi.

15 Benevolence and righteousness are two of the Virues in the Code of Bushido.

The Dokkōdō

Although, as has been indicated, Miyamoto Musashi did not write The Samurai Creed, he did in fact author a number of significant writings that are still timely today. The first, of course, is his classic **Go Rin-no-Sho**, or *Book of Five Rings*, Musashi's venerated tome on strategy written under the guise of a sword manual. It is, however, his lesser-known advice on living that interests us here.

The **Dokkōdō**, variously translatd as *The Way Alone*, *The Way to Go Forth Alone*, or *The Way of Walking Alone*, is a short work written by Musashi the week before he died in 1645. Its list of twenty-one precepts were prepared as a final letter to his favorite disciple, Terao Magonojō. They represents the sword master's counsel on how to live a stringent but righteous and honest life. Anyone who is forced, or chooses, to walk alone will discover great value in, and allow them to develop a truth within you.

The Way Alone

1. *Accept everything just the way it is.*
2. *Do not seek pleasure for its own sake.*
3. *Do not give preference to anything among all things.*
4. *Think lightly of yourself and deeply of the world.*
5. *Be detached from desire your whole life.*
6. *Do not regret what you have done.*
7. *Never be jealous.*
8. *Never let yourself be saddened by a separation.*
9. *Resentment and complaint are appropriate neither for oneself nor others.*
10. *Do not let yourself be guided by the feeling of lust or love.*
11. *Do not seek elegance and beauty in all things.*
12. *Be indifferent to where you live.*
13. *Do not pursue the taste of good food.*
14. *Do not hold on to possessions you no longer need.*
15. *Do not act following customary beliefs.*
16. *Do not collect weapons or practice with weapons beyond what is useful.*
17. *Do not fear death.*
18. *Do not seek to possess either goods or fiefs for your old age.*
19. *Respect Buddha and the gods without counting on their help.*
20. *You may abandon your own body but you must preserve your honor.*
21. *Never depart from the Way[16] [of the Martial Arts.]*

Whether one follows the *Samurai Creed* of anonymous provenance, the *Dokkodo* of Miyamoto Musashi, or some other relevant set of tenets, it should be one that bolsters body, mind, and spirit as an integrated whole. Integrity, as will be seen in the next section, is what keeps us fundamentally whole and comporting ourselves in full alignment with our goals and objectives.

---

16 Musashi's use of the term *Way* refers as much to the concept of the *Tao*, as to the concept of *michi*, or "life path."

KATSURA OTOKO—A TEST OF SHINOBI

The Nakano School provided a rigorous introduction to the life of an agent. Extended courses were provided on a wide variety of topics including languages, philosophy, history, current events, martial arts, propaganda, counter intelligence and the facets of covert action.

—WB Simpson,
Special Agent in the Pacific

Though some today may be tempted to dismiss the ninjutsu's concept of *katsura otoko* as an archaic tactic, its worth and significance was proven to be as relevant in WWII as it was during the golden age of ninjutsu. The best-documented example of *katsura otoko* during that period was Second Lieutenant Hiroo Onoda, who served in the Imperial Japanese Army. His exploits throughout his three decades of solitary existence[17] are documented in his book, **No Surrender: My Thirty Year War**, which is mandatory reading for anyone who purports to walk the path of the shinobi.

The Imperial Japanese Army's Shinobi Academy

After graduating from officers training school with honors, Onoda was surprised to have been selected to receive further training at the Futamata branch of the **Rikugun Nakano Gakko**—the *Nakano School of Secret Warfare.* In **Japanese Intelligence in World War II**, Ken Kotani describes this military school for spies as follows:

> *The objective of the Nakano School was the rapid training of officers who, mainly engaging in counter-sedition work and information-gathering, would fight the covert war, which the*

---

17 Onoda began his decades of isolated existence with three other comrades, but these intermittently succumbed to the vicissitudes of jungle life over the course of time.

school defined as consisting of espionage, propaganda, security, and plots ... Other elements of its education were as follows: "knowledge" subjects such as foreign languages, war studies, conspiracy, and intelligence; practical subjects such as kendo, judo, and ciphers; fieldwork, etc.

In a 1995 **Studies in Intelligence** file, declassified by the CIA in 2007, Stephen Mercado reported,

The campus featured halls where students honed their skills at traditional fencing (kendo) and such martial arts as aikido. Ninja masters were invited to impart their ancient secrets. Instructors drummed into students the spirit of endurance against all hardships to execute their missions.

Upon completion of his military-sponsored covert activities curriculum, Onoda was deployed to lead a contingent of Japanese guerrilla forces in a remote area of the Philippines. The final orders he received from his squadron commander, Major **Yoshimi Taniguchi**, underscored the *katsura otoko* nature of Onoda's secret warfare mission:

You are absolutely forbidden to die by your own hand. It may take three years, it may take five, but whatever happens, we'll come back for you. Until then, so long as you have one soldier, you are to continue to lead him. You may have to live on coconuts. If that's the case, live on coconuts! Under no circumstances are you [to] give up your life voluntarily

The Essence of Shinobi

The accepted notion that Onoda's thirty-year struggle was based on his belief that the war had not ended is refuted by William Webb, in his book, **Seven Japanese WWII Soldiers Who Refused to Surrender After the War**. The book recounts the experiences Japanese soldiers—

Onoda and six others—who remained faithful to the orders from the start of their service to well after the war had ended. Webb observes,

> *The standard interpretation is that Onoda refused to believe the war was over and that is why he continued fighting. This is not true. Onoda surely knew the war was over, the demoralized troops and the "wishful thinking" of their officers he encountered when he arrived at Lubang surely gave him his first indication of that. However, his guerrilla [sic] training had taught him that a war is never lost until the last soldier gives up fighting.*

Both at the end of Major Taniguchi's quote and the one above, in Webb's last sentence, we note an emphasis on one overriding tenet: *Never give up!* It is a tenet that stated in positive terms becomes the mandate encompassed by the *kanji* **nin**: Persist. Persevere. Endure!

Elsewhere, Mercado reports,

> *Major Ito, a skilled swordsman ruomred to have cut down over 80 guerrillas and spies in Manchuria during the IJA[18] takeover in 1931, had first opposed creating the Nakano School. Once appointed to oversee the training there, however, he dedicated himself to drilling into its students a "spiritual" education ... Instructors drummed into students the spirit of endurance against all hardships to execute their missions.*

This ideology was fully in keeping with the teachings of the Nakano School which, as Ken Kotani cites:

> *By investing in ideological education, the school could nurture intelligence officers who would be resistant to bribery or honey traps and would fight through the Pacific War under terrible conditions ...*

---

18 Imperial Japanese Army

A Testament to Katsura Otoko

In the face of such ideological conviction, it is easy to understand Onoda's enduring allegiance to his training, his beliefs, and his country. The rationale he describes is predictably identical to the ideological objectives cited by Kotani. In Onoda's words:

> When I became a soldier, I accepted my country's goals. I vowed that I would do anything within my power to achieve those goals ... having been born male and Japanese, I considered it my sacred duty, once I had passed the army physical examination, to become a soldier and fight for Japan.

It is a testament to his belief systems that Onoda remained isolated on the Philippines island of Lubang for twenty-nine years after the end of World War II. Of necessity, practical ninjutsu demands a certain level of paranoia and due to this Onoda resisted multiple of attempts from family, friends, and the Japanese government to give up his fight when the war was over. It was not until 1972 the Onoda finally emerged from the Lubang jungles and surrendered his katana to Philippines President Ferdinand Marcos.

In **No Surrender**, Onoda recalls how the training he received at the *Rikugun Nakano Gakko* prepared the secret warfare trainees for potential dilemma. He writes:

> "In what, then, can those engaged in this kind of warfare place their hope? The Nakano Military School answered this question with a simple sentence: 'In secret warfare, there is integrity.'
> "And this is right, for integrity is the greatest necessity when a man must deceive not only his enemies but his friends[19].

---

19 That is, of course, because a spy cannot reveal to those around him that he is a spy. How many ninjutsu practitioners today can be said to follow this fundamental tenet of ninjutsu?

With integrity—and in this I include sincerity, loyalty, devotion to duty and a sense of morality—one can withstand all hardships and ultimately turn hardship itself into victory. This was a lesson that the instructors at Futamaata were constantly trying to instill in us."

Without the requisite understanding of integrity and commitment as his guiding philosophy, the isolated shinobi agent can easily come to despair and begin questioning his mission, his motives, and his very being. With the requisite understanding of his art's overriding principles, on the other hand, the shinobi agent is able to persevere and withstand even the most demoralizing obstacles. And that, after all, is the ultimate significance of the character *nin*. Those two attributes then, integrity and endurance, will be requisites for the ninjutsu practitioner operating as *katsura otoko*.

Onoda Hiroo surrenders his *Gunto* to Ferdinand Marcos, 1978

Part II:

The Psychological Components

桂男

What Taijutsu? — Hands and Feet are Last Resort!

GOSHIN-NO-SANPO

It is significant to note that the unit motto of the Rikugun Nakano Gakko—the "spy school" that trained what were arguably the last body of military shinobi operatives of the 20th century—was *"Success in clandestine activity comes from integrity."*

To authentically espouse *Shinobi-no-Michi*, it is critical to understand and adhere to its core tenets; and while it can be difficult to prioritize the tenets in a meaningful sequence, there can be little doubt that among the most imperative ones for the *shinobi* is the concept of **Banpen Fugyo**. This tenet reminds us that:

> *No one possesses the knowledge concerning the events of tomorrow. This means that we do not know when our life will cease. However, you should not be surprised by any kind of happening. Whether a change in the divine process occurs, a cutting action is attempted by an opponent, or natural catastrophes take place, you should never feel such a thing as surprise. This is the spirit of Banpen fugyo.*

> **Banpen** *means "change," and* **fugyo**, *"never surprised". What one should have in mind, first of all, is caring for one's own life; this is common sense. Health, both physical and spiritual, is needed in order to prevent accidents. Due to the impetuousness of the youth I made lots of errors until the age of forty. Now, every morning I massage myself using an ice cold towel and go with my dog for a walk. After that, I dedicate some time to painting and writing. Those who are evil-minded will always do bad things. Even the bad intentioned ninja should be banished. This is applicable to any martial system.*

The concept of Banpen Fugyo is discussed in great depth elsewhere; what is important now is knowing how to abide by it. For this, we can begin the *Three Laws of Personal Protection* we call the **Goshin-no-Sanpo**.

Law One: **Never Hurt Yourself**

This law means a shinobi must deliberately avoid any action, activity, concept, or opportunity that in any way may cause him harm or diminish his personal standards, whether mentally, physically, emotionally, or spiritually.

On first glance this law may seem a bit obvious and simple. It is my experience, however, that many times the obvious may not be quite as simple as you might think. Never hurt yourself is our first Law because it is often the First Law to be broken.

The concept of *never hurt yourself*, for our purposes, covers two areas: *firstly* is **the application of techniques**. Every available caution should be taken to learn and practice each basic and exercise correctly and safely. *Shinobi* should all be aware of their own limits when practicing bujutsu. Taijutsu, jujutsu, and other martial arts training systems often include high impact exercises. These techniques and basics, even when executed correctly, put generous amounts of strain on joints and muscles. Jumping, kicking, punching, and the various exercises necessary to develop skill in personal protectioncan and do tax a body to its limits. It is the responsibility of the *shinobi* to be constantly aware of his personal abilities.

Secondly are **the personal applications**. It is important for *shinobi* to remember that he is a total person. Activities such as drug and alcohol abuse, violent behavior, poor health maintainance, and other detrimental practices should be avoided. Shinobi will often find that *an attitude of self-respect* will serve as the best form of defense. Anyone who practices this First Law in everyday situations can learn to reach higher and do more than others by learning to value oneself.

Law Two: **The Best Protection is to Avoid Being Attacked**

This law refers to the *Strategy of Defense*. First it should be understood that avoidance of dangerous situations is the best defense. It is the hope of our instructors that all shinobi practice the proper judgment in determining what may be the appropriate action taken in each personal protectionsituation. It is, often, more important that a shinobi know when to fight rather than how to fight. Avoiding an attack means to avoid situations of conflict or vulnerability.

Second, avoiding an attack refers to the physical applications of personal protection techniques. Side stepping and hip rotations are easy and effective ways to avoid an oncoming attack. It is the purpose of this strategy to enable a skilled shinobi to protect himself from injury while expending the least possible energy. This tactic reserves the most possible energy for the shinobi to use in his counterattack. By allowing an opponent to tire himself in useless attempts at harm, a skilled shinobi may limit the amount of force required to diffuse the attack. The end result is limited injury for both the attacker and the shinobi.

Law Three: **Always Be Prepared**

All shinobi recognize the vital importance of three personal attributes —*foresight*, *preparedness*, and **vigilance**. Foresight derives from the understanding of *banpen fugyo*; vigilance derives from the unceasing practice of foresight; and preparedness is the inevitable outcome of exercising foresight and remaining ever vigilant.

Moreover, it is the responsibility of every shinobi to routinely hone their acquired body of strategies, tactics, and techniques to the point where these are functional. A shinobi must study a wide variety of subjects in an effort to prepare the mind for quick thinking. A skilled shinobi can accurately assess unintended signals from an adversary and intuitively respond with an appropriate strategy.

The most successful shinobi are those who proactively train for and develop new countermeasures for potential or imminent situations. They are careful never to stagnate, and constantly seek new options or opportunities for addressing conditions that may loom on the horizon. Any advantage missed or disregarded violates the first Law of Personal Protection—*Never Hurt Yourself.* Not being proactive is tantamount to not being foresighted and constitutes a lapse in one of the three requisite shinobi attributes.

These are the basic concepts of *Personal Protection*. Follow them and you will realize your potential. Disregard them and you will leave a lesser student than when you arrived.

SHINGAKURE

Ninjutsu has been described to be the *art of invsibility*, and its exponents, by extension, the invisible operatives. At the New York Ninpokai the aspect of invisibility—or *Onshinjutsu*—is one of the many *Kugei* disciplines we acknowledge as being indispensible to the practice of Ninjutsu. Quite simply, an enemy can attempt to counter or stop a perceived threat—but it's difficult for him to defend against a threat he doesn't know exists. Whether used for personal security, intelligence-gathering, espionage, or some other laudible or nefarious end, the art and its practitioners rely on invisibility, or at least on *controlling*, *altering*, and *manipulating* others' perceptions. In other words, *virtually* invisible.For the *shoshinsha*, or novice *shinobi*, training in **Onshinjutsu** begins at the fundamental level—*by erasing the ego*. Not completely, of course, but enough of it so that he doesn't get slighted, offended, or upset at the insults that lead egotistical people into trouble.

He is thus introduced to the First Law of Ninjutsu: ***mugei-mumei*** (or, "no art, no name.") By stressing the importance of *anonymity* to the novice, the two aspects of his life that potentially create the greatest sense of pride for him—his *skill*[20] and his *identity*[21]—are removed from his ego. His reactions then begin to be more rationale and less (or *not at all*) emotional.

---

20 Or *art.*
21 Or *name.*

Shingakure—Hiding in your Enemy's Mind

With the gradual suppression of his ego, the novice can immerse himself fully into his training, *without* the self-conscious preoccupations for *how he looks, what others think,* and other *counterproductive concerns* that negatively affect performance and learning. Without the culturally-induced ego investment, skill development tends to accelerate. At that point, the physical arts of invisibility can be introduced into the training.

The infiltration art of **Shinobi-iri** will teach him what makes noise during movement, and how to lessen or eliminate it when walking, crawling, running, and jumping. **Intonpo** will teach him how to plan his escapes and disappearances before he needs them. **Gotonpo** will teach him how and where to hide in his environment when *intonpo* methods fail or are unavailable. The proper use of **tonki**, or distraction tools, will enable him to befudddle pursuers as he effects his escape or disappearance. However, these and many other physical methods of invisibility will come in time, *when his body is disciplined.* For now, he will learn to become "invisible" using mental disciplines by using the Nine Tenets for *Hiding in the Enemy's Mind.*

Nine Tenets of Deception

Although traditional ninjutsu provides its practitioners with an innumerable variety of strategies and tactics for "not being seen, heard, or perceived,"—*shinobi-iri*, *intonpo*; *gotonpo*, and so forth—at the core of such methods is an understanding of human nature, and of the base motivations common to all men, whether they are regarded as foes or friends, enemies or allies. It is this understanding of human nature, and its near-universal motivations, that allow the *shinobi* practitioner to act and remain unperceived and undetected in plain sight of others, even in the absence of his elaborate deceptions and unimagineable equipment.

The successful application of the Nine Tenets is only possible if the shinobi has unreservedly adopted the concept of *mugei-mumei*. Any vestige of ego will negate the usefulness of the Tenets and sabotage their efficacy. Below is a set of nine timeless ninjutsu tenets that have been adeptly utilized by the *shinobi* in effectively controlling, altering, and manipulating the perceptions of those around him.

Tenet No. 1: **Assume Formlessness**
By taking a shape, or having a visible plan, you open yourself to attack. Instead of taking a form for your enemy to grasp, keep yourself adaptable and on the move. Accept the fact that nothing is certain and no tenet is fixed. The best way to protect yourself is to be as fluid and formless as water; never bet on stability or lasting order. Everything changes.

Tenet No. 2: **Conceal Your Intentions**

Keep people off-balance and in the dark by never revealing the purpose behind your actions. If they have no clue what you are up to, they cannot prepare a defense. Guide them far enough down the wrong path, envelope them in enough smoke, and by the time they realize your intentions, it will be too late.

Tenet No. 3: **Pose as a Friend to Work as a Spy**

Knowing about your rival is critical. Use spies to gather valuable information that will keep you a step ahead. Better still: Play the spy yourself. In polite social encounters, learn to probe. Ask indirect questions to get people to reveal their weaknesses and intentions. There is no occasion that is not an opportunity for artful spying.

Tenet No. 4: **Seem Less Knowedgeable than Your Adversary**

No one likes feeling stupider than the next persons. The trick, is to make your victims feel smart – and not just smart, but smarter than you are. Once convinced of this, they will never suspect that you may have ulterior motives.

Tenet No. 5: **Think as You Like But Behave Like Others**

If you make a show of going against the times, flaunting your unconventional ideas and unorthodox ways, people will think that you only want attention and that you look down upon them. They will find a way to punish you for making them feel inferior. It is far safer to blend in and nurture the common touch. Share your originality only with tolerant friends and those who are sure to appreciate your uniqueness.

Tenet No. 6: **Disarm Enemies with the Mirror Effect**
The mirror reflects reality, but it is also the perfect tool for deception: When you mirror your enemies, doing exactly as they do, they cannot figure out your strategy. The Mirror Effect mocks and humiliates them, making them overreact. By holding up a mirror to their psyches, you seduce them with the illusion that you share their values; by holding up a mirror to their actions, you teach them a lesson. Few can resist the power of Mirror Effect.

Tenet No. 7: **Make your Accomplishments Seem Effortless**
Your actions must seem natural and executed with ease. All the toil and practice that go into them, and also all the clever tricks, must be concealed. When you act, act effortlessly, as if you could do much more. Avoid the temptation of revealing how hard you work – it only raises questions. Reveal your metods to no one or they will be used against you.

Tenet No. 8: **Cultivate an Air of Unpredictability**
Humans are creatures of habit with an insatiable need to see familiarity in other people's actions. Your predictability gives them a sense of control. Turn the tables: Be deliberately unpredictable. Behavior that seems to have no consistency or purpose will keep them offbalance, and they will wear themselves out trying to explain your moves. Taken to an extreme, this strategy can intimidate and terrorize.

Avoid Suspicion by Safeguarding Your Reputation

Tenet No. 9: **Avoid Suspicion by Safeguarding Your Reputation**

Reputation is the cornerstone of power. Through reputation alone you can intimidate and win; once you slip, however, you are vulnerable, and will be attacked on all sides. Make your reputation unassailable. Always be alert to potential attacks and thwart them before they happen. Meanwhile, learn to destroy your enemies by opening holes in their own reputations. Then stand aside and let public opinion hang them.

The *Nine Tenets of Deception* were originally passed down verbally, in traditional *okuden* manner, without details or explanations. The brief commentaries accompanying the ones above were added later and, in fact, remain unnecessary. This is because even as simple phrases, the Tenets have been effectively applied against political and military enemies from the time of Sonbu. Their use predates the practice of Ninjutsu and the birth of modern-day intelligence tradecraft, although the shinobi and contemporary espionage agents are versed in their use.

Caveat

It is necessary to remember that the term *Nine Tenets of Deception* is an archaic misnomer, as their utility goes well beyond the strategy of deception, and their subtle but practiced use can serve as a tool for infiltration, invisibility, and safe return without the potential for discovery, exposure, or retaliation. As such, they represent a golden skeleton key that can open all doors for the *shinobi* with the requisite mindset.

ONSHINJUTSU

The ultimate skill is to take up a position where you are formless. If you are formless, the most penetrating spies will not be able to discern you, or the wisest counsels will not be able to do calculations against you.

—Sonbu
Sonshi

The way of the *shinobi* has been interpreted to be many things by many people. The *Art of Stealth*, the *Art of Espionage*, the *Art of Assassination*, and the *Art of Protection Against Danger* are among the most-often heard interpretations. Certainly ninjutsu encompasses all of these skills and more, being an art that provides the practitioner with an unlimited variety of strategies and philosophies for coping with the various forms of conflict encountered in life.

Some interpretations mistakenly stress the physical aspects of ninjutsu, while others, just as erroneously, overemphasize the esoteric. All are impressive. But perhaps the most dramatic interpretation of ninjutsu is that of the *Art of Invisibility*. Still, invisibility, like every other interpretation of the way of the *shinobi*, is merely a sub-system of this comprehensive ancient art. More accurately, when one speaks of invisibility one is referring to the shinobi art of *onshinjutsu*.

Onshinjutsu, literally the *art of concealing oneself in front of others*, relies on techniques of distraction, suggestion, camouflage, and deception in order to give an observer the impression that either the *shinobi* does not exist or that he has disappeared. Like ninjutsu, the art that fostered it, onshinjutsu is also made up of many sub-arts which, when practiced collectively, allow the *shinobi* to vanish from his opponent's sight under a variety of circumstances. Furthermore, the diversity of these sub-arts that comprise the art of onshinjutsu allow the practice of invisibility to be manifested, like the parent art of ninjutsu, on a physical, mental, and metaphysical level.

The Physical Level

On the purely physical level of invisibility there exist the arts of tonpo and inpo (respectively translated, the "way of hiding" and the "way of escaping".) Using tonpo methods the *shinobi* avails himself of his environment to cloak his presence within it. Structures, natural objects and the existing urban or rural landscape are adapted to in ways that permit him to blend and merge with his surroundings.

Tonpo

Mastery of tonpo requires arduous training in body discipline and muscle control, particularly in the limbs. Long hours of practice are necessary so that the *shinobi* can contour and contort his body to conform with a multitude of shapes in a given environment. His body may have to assume an oval form in order to crowd behind a small boulder. It may have to adopt an angular, disjointed position to blend with the jagged patterns of barren tree branches. Or it may simply be forced to maintain a painfully still position, such as pressing flat against a building's buttress or hanging suspended from a window ledge without the benefit of iron claws or harnesses, until such time as it is safe enough to continue onward.

Goemon Ishikawa disappears from pursuers using Tonpo

Inpo

Inpo escaping methods depend more on the ever-popular shinobi gadgetry found in his bag of tricks than on the shinobi's actual body skills (although skill with the gadgetry is a pre-requisite for their proper utillization). Foremost among the shinobi's array of invisibility and evasion aids are the metsubushi and gantsubushi blinding substances. These "sight removers" are more often than not meant to have only a temporary effect on the opponent, since the shinobi is quite proficient at disappearing in the proverbial wink of an eye.

Metsubushi

Ancient metsubushi substances could be found in the form of powders, liquids, light, smoke and explosives. The substances could also be combined to create itching, choking or burning sensations to accompany the "blinding." Pepper mixed with metal filings is a good example of a powder-type metsubushi. Onion juice was a shinobi favorite as far as liquids were concerned.

Blinding light could be the focused intensity of the sun's rays reflected from a mirror-polished surface. Smoke was not only used for disappearing but, alternately, it could also serve as a screen enabling the shinobi to undetectedly penetrate an enemy perimeter. And minor explosives comparable to firecrackers could be tossed at a pursuer's face, affording the shinobi the opportunity to advance or retreat without his opponent being the wiser.

Kagi-nawa

Ropes with small hooks attached at one end, called kagi-nawa, were also an indispensable part of the ancient shinobi's *inpo* accessories. With enough lead time, the hook and line permitted the pursued shinobi to climb or descend to a higher or lower level than that of his pursuers. He could climb out of a dead end alley or other *cul-de-sac* before his enemies' arrival, making it seem that he had vanished into thin air. Or he could lower himself from a roof to a window or courtyard, again giving the impression of having disappeared and lending credence to the belief that he could dematerialize at will.

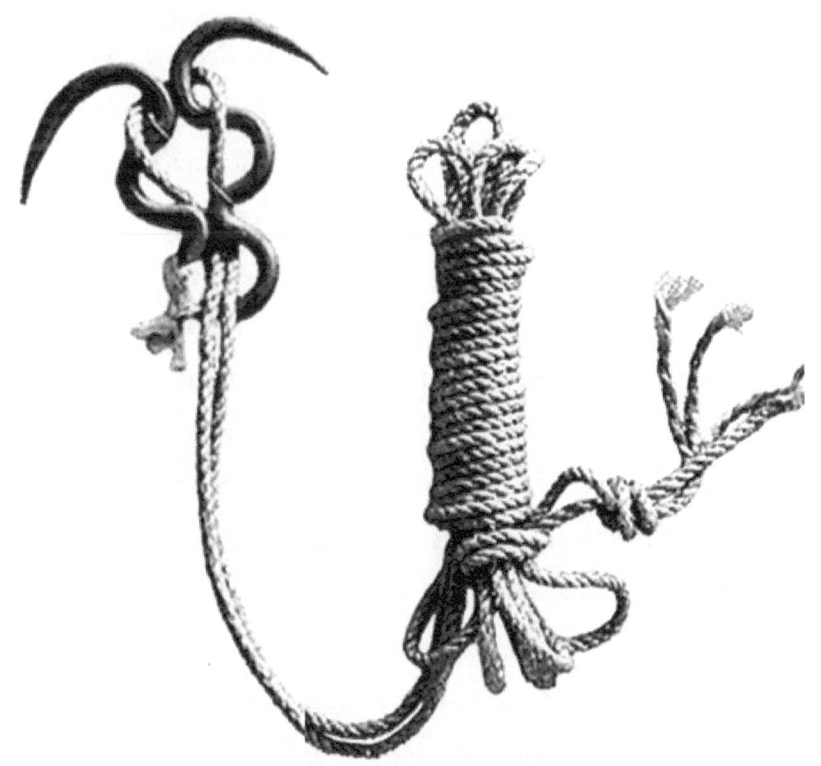

The *Kagi-nawa*, A Tool for Getting In—or Getting Out

The Mental Level

The mental level of onshinjutsu employs the power of suggestion and misdirection in much the same manner that a magician utilizes these skills to deceive his audience. As a basic example, a shinobi might throw a rock or coin in a direction opposite his actual location in an effort to cause an alert sentry to leave his post, giving the shinobi free access to the controlled area. He can use a decoy shinobi, instead of a thrown rock, to the same end, Or he may resort to the use of disguise and impersonation, assuming the identity of another to, again, pass and enter "invisibly" and undetected. This is known as **henso-jutsu**.

The Spy as Actor

The mental aspects of invisibility having to do with decoys and diversions require only minimal skill coupled with minimal imagination to be successful. Resorting to disguise and impersonation is a riskier undertaking, as well as a more difficult one. Although the assumption of a role is often short-term in duration, it nevertheless requires the *shinobi* to intensely study to "become" the type of character he will be representing himself as. Here the *shinobi* is not so much a spy as an actor, although there is not that much difference between the two functions. In essence, they are the same. Whether as spy or actor, the *shinobi* is a person being seen as someone he is not. His true self goes unperceived and thus he is "invisible". Make-up and wardrobe in this respect are not as important as attitude projected. Cosmetics and credentials are never as important as conviction. Total immersion in the assumed role is vital to disguising not only your true self but, more significantly, your true intentions.

At this point it becomes obvious that the key to the mental aspect of invisibility is not the quality of "not being there" but rather, not being whom you appear to be. This has always been the secret to successful espionage. The ancient shinobi discovered this and Japan's modern day shinobi agents continue the practice. Intelligence specialist Richard Deacon wrote the following about the Japanese Secret Service:

> "...Occasionally Japanese Intelligence in action has been so blatantly daring and obvious that it has not been recognized for what it is. At other times it has kept so low a profile that the more complacent bureaucrats of the other secret services have been foolish enough to propound that Japan never had an effective Intelligence organization..."

Thus, one may safely conclude that the shinobi's degree of invisibility is contingent upon his effectiveness in the portrayal of his projected "self"; in his suggestion of friendship when, in truth, there is enmity; in his facade of a simpleton while he schemes and manipulates; in his apparent complacency as he quietly sows conspiracy and subversion. Perceiving the shinobi as innocuous is the gravest error his opponent can make. Treacherous? Perhaps. But if the ancient shinobi learned a lesson from their Jesuit enemies in the fifteenth century, it was the quasi-theological precept "the ends justify the means."

The Metaphysical Level

The metaphysical level of onshinjutsu is at once the subtlest to use and the most difficult to master. Invisibility on this highest of levels demands total suppression of the self in order to undergo a situation unperceived, without benefit of ruse deception, disguise, or artifice.

Furthermore, it must be "performed" unconsciously since a conscious effort is the surest way of failing to achieve it. To get an idea as to what it means to become invisible by suppressing the self, attempt the following: the next time you spot a friend in a crowded urban environment, walk up to him and tap him on the chest before he sees you.

Under normal circumstances this will be difficult if you approach him frontally because your physical characteristics and your psychic self will be recognizable to your friend. When you next see him, consciously begin disregarding him as a person or an object as you approach. Commit your body to walk right "through" him.

You should notice that you were able to approach closer to him this time before he recognized you. On subsequent encounters, turn this personal disregard inward as if you don't exist. Don't think of yourself as a nonperson; simply disregard your physical and mental existence. By drawing your psychic self inward you suppress the familiar projections that make you recognizable to those who know you. Your goal is to become faceless in a crowd. You'll know you've succeeded when closest friends walk right past you.

Charisma and Animal Magnetism

Although the practice of invisibility on the metaphysical level is almost exclusively the province of the *shinobi* it is also one of the most difficult skills for him to attain. This is because any individual who practices a high degree of physical and mental discipline exudes a form of aura that is noticeable when they enter a room. This attention-drawing quality is often simplistically referred to as "bearing" or "character." Certain athletes possess it. So do many politicians, as well as ballerinas and other performing artists. Some call it charisma; others, animal magnetism. The quality defies semantics.

The Epitome of Invisibility

This perceptible presence is also distinguishable in highly accomplished martial artists. Bruce Lee was a good was a good example of this. In such cases, this nonverbal communication of total body discipline is a bonus, alerting potential troublemakers to keep away. It does not, however, benefit the exponent of ninjutsu who strives to draw as little attention to himself as possible, and who wants to be remenbered by few, if any. Yet due to the nature of his training, the *shinobi* is inevitably heir to this aura. He must therefore make a deliberate attempt to eschew this inherent perceptibility.

How? The answer with which most scholars of ninjutsu agree is by controlling his method of walking, as already noted by Jay Gluck in **Zen Combat**:

> "...The ninja must never swagger. His walk is light, straight and swift, appearing by remaining unnoticed. A master of this walk finds it easy to become a human chameleon, to blend with the motion around him, or the motionlessness."

This all-pervasive nature of being like a chameleon, of being unseen in the best of places, is then the epitome of the *art of invisibility*.

The late Yumio Nawa,
researcher, writer,
and reknown master
of Ninjutsu,
Juttejutsu, Hojojutsu,
and Shurikenjutsu

... as well as many of the
lost ways, including
Shinobi Aruki,
the special stealthy steps
of the Ninja

Part III:

The Physical Component

桂
男

Attitude, Breath, Gaze, Balance, Distance, and Spatial Perception

BUKYO—PRINCIPLES OF ENGAGEMENT

Your *posture*; your *breath management*; your *combat gaze*; your skill at *breaking an adversary's mental and physical equilibrium*; your control of the *engagement distance*; and your adeptness at *reading and responding to the enemy's unspoken intentions* are known collectively as **Bukyo**, or universal *Principles of Personal Engagement*. The *bukyo* principles apply to personal combat regardlerss of modality, whether it take place with sword, firearms, or the empty hand.

At the early stages of training for combative personal engage-ments, we learn and acquire the fundamentals of cutting, thrusting, aiming, shooting, punching, or kicking, all of which take varying lengths of time to do well. At the later stages, our focus must progress to the universal principles below, which will allow us to use our acquired first stage knowledge in a variety conflict situations—not merely combative encounters—when contending with a broad range of adversaries, opponents, or enemies.

KAMAE

Kamae is a Japanese term used in martial arts, as well as in traditional theater. It translates approximately to *posture*. The *kanji* of this word means base. Kamae is to be differentiated from the word **tachi**, used in Japanese martial arts to mean **stance**. While *tachi* (pronounced *dachi* when used in a compound) refers to the position of the body from the waist down, **kamae** refers to the posture of the *entire body*, as well as encompassing *one's mental posture* (i.e., one's *attitude*). These connected mental and physical aspects of readiness may be referred to individually as *kokoro-gamae* and mi-gamae, respectively.

Although it is a generic term, context may mean there's a default specific posture which is being implicitly referred to. e.g. many modern styles use kamae by itself as shorthand usually for the style's basic stance for sparring or self-defense. As a further note, there are also related verbs, and adding *te* to the end of *kamae* makes the command for "get ready/in position" (*kamaete).*

KOKYU

Kokyu is the Japanese term for **breath power**, but the proper use of kokyu refers to much more than lung capacity. It involves utilization of *the entire body*. It is not simply breath, but the concentrated *power that arises when body and mind are unified*. Breath power is crucial in the **bugei**. Even if one's lung capacity is not increased, one can still attain great and liberating power through unification of body and mind.

Focusing on breathing is vital in combat because it is one of the few activities in which the conscious and subconsious merge. In other words, you can control your breathing with your conscious mind or just let your body conduct it by itself. By observing your breathing closely, you start to have a better idea of the relationship between your conscious and subconscious mind, as well as how both are affecting other aspects of your physical activity. Your attack is usually most effective when you time it with your exhalation. By extension, you should be inhaling when drawing someone else's attack into your circle so you can throw the energy back out wheh you exhale.

Breath power and *ki* are the sources of *bugei* strength. There are no human beings who do not breathe, and everyone does it unconsciously. If breathing ceases, we will quickly depart from this world. Breathing is the most natural of reflexes. *Ki* and breath power are indivisible and are the very being of bugei.

METSUKE

Metsuke means *combat gaze* and in combat it means where you look during an engagement. *Metsuke* not only helps you see what your opponent is doing or going to do, but it *also gives your opponent information about you.* Even if you feel scared on the inside, you should have a steady, confident gaze that doesn't give anything away to your opponent.

During training you should always imagine your opponent and look at where their eyes would be. You shouldn't be looking at the ground. Occasionally look at your feet to check your footwork but other than that, look straight ahead.

Against an Opponent

Look straight at your opponent to project your confidence. By looking away or at the ground, your opponent will gain confidence because they know his presence is having a strong effect on you. Some traditions say you should look directly at your opponent's eyes. Other traditions warn that looking at the eyes can be mesmerising and that one should instead look at the whole person from head to toe.

Metsuke and Facial Expressions

Your facial expression can give your opponent as much information about your state of mind as your metsuke. Generally, people who pull exaggerated faces during engagement are not that effective. The most effective facial expression is just your *natural, calm face*. No matter what happens, your face stays serene. This is much more unsettling for an opponent than an angry war face, and it is much less tiring for you. A calm face it helps you to stay calm, and in turn helps you to observe your opponent, because you are not wasting effort attempting to decieve him. However, if your are fully intent on vanquishing your opponent, your calm face will naturally take on a piercing and intense quality. Your opponent will get this understanding, as well.

KUZUSHI

Kuzushi is a Japanese term in the martial arts for *breaking or disrupting an opponent's balance*. The noun comes from the intransitive verb, *kuzusu*, meaning to *level, pull down*, or *demolish*[22]. As such, it is refers to not just an unbalancing, but the *process* of getting an opponent into a position where his stability, and hence ability to regain compromised balance, is destroyed. *Kuzushi* is important to many styles of Japanese martial arts, especially those derived from, or influenced by, Jujutsu training methods. In taijutsu / jujutsu, it is

---

22 Not the opponent; just his sense of balance.

considered an essential principle and the first of three stages to a successful throwing technique; that is, *kuzushi, tsukuri* (fitting or entering), and *kake* (execution).

The methods of effecting *kuzushi* depend on **maai** (combative distance) and other circumstances. It can be achieved using **tai sabaki** (body displacement or evasion), taking advantage of the opponents actions[23], **atemi** (strikes), or a combination of all three. There are three primary ways of applying kuzushi in close-quarter combat:

1. *direct action* (e.g. pulling or pushing while entering for a throw);
2. *inducing opponent's action* (e.g. a feint or combination attack);
3. *direct action by opponent* (e.g. a counter throw).

MAAI

Maai translating simply to *interval*, is a Japanese martial arts term referring to *the space between two opponents* in combat; formally, *the engagement distance*. It is a complex concept, incorporating not just the distance between opponents, but also *the time it will take to cross the distance, angle,* and *rhythm of attack*. It is specifically the *exact position from which one opponent can strike the other*, after factoring in the above elements.

For example, a faster opponent's *maai* is farther away than a slower opponent. It is ideal for one opponent to maintain *maai* while preventing the other from doing so, meaning that they can strike

---

23 Example, push when pulled, pull when pushed.

before the opponent can (rather than both striking simultaneously, or being struck without being able to strike back).

In *kenjutsu*, *maai* has a more specific interpretation. In physical terms it pertains to the distance *maintained* between two opponents. When *maai* is interpreted as the actual distance between opponents, there are three types:

- *Tō-ma* — long distance
- **Issoku ittō-no-maai** (or just, **Itto-ma**) — one-foot-one-sword distance, also called **chūma** — middle distance
- **Chika-ma** — short distance

Itto-ma is the distance equaling one step to make one strike. It measures about seven feet (two metres) between opponents; from which either need advance only one step in order to strike the other. Normally, most techniques are initiated at this distance.

Chika-ma is the distance narrower than *Itto-ma* (short/close distance), and To-ma is greater (long/far distance). At *To-ma*, there is a small margin of time to allow for a reaction to be made against an opponent's attack. But at *Issoku itto-no-ma* there exists almost no margin at all, so that at this distance one's attention has to remain constantly alert and unbroken.

Timing

In terms of time, *maai* pertains to the momentary lapses of awareness that are manifested in the opponent's mind. Extended further, it also embraces the concept of **Kyo-jitsu** (emptiness-fullness of *ki*). These momentary lapses of mind, and *Kyo-jitsu*, we may call the **kokoro-no-maai** (mental interval). The implication of *kokoro-no-maai* is that although the physical distance between opponents may be mutually advantageous, the mental interval possessed by individuals will determine who will have the decisive advantage.

MUSUBI

Musubi is the study of good "communication." In any potential encounter between individuals, whether combative or otherwise, *communication* exists, regardless of it being acknowledged or not. It is up to the individuals in the interaction to determine whether the communication will be productive or useless, friendly or hostile, true or inaccurate. **Musubi**, as it is refined over time, can mean *the ability to control and alter interaction*, changing a hostile approach to a healthy encounter or an attack into a handshake.

Another important feature of *musubi* is operating in your encounter on that crowded street. As you meet the pedestrian who is walking toward you, your reactions reflect and respond to the other person's, rather than conflicting with them. The conjunction of you and the other pedestrian represents a continuous and smooth *flow of energy*, a give and take of force and direction. This is another, and perhaps the most important, element of musubi—namely, learning to feel and use the energy.

KURAI DORI

Attack is the secret of defense: defense is the planning of an attack.
—Sonbu
Sonshi, Chapter Six

Most self-defense situations and attack scenarios *issue rays of prior warning* if you are perceptive enough to spot the attacker's ritual. If you are foolhardy enough to heighten your vulnerability by placing yourself in a dangerous situation (like walking down a dark alley at night) you cannot expect any prior warning and will have to make the best of a bad situation. You then fall into the ambush attack. Most people in society are so **switched off**, both mentally and environmentally, that many attack scenarios fall into the ambush variety. If this is so, and it so often is, you will be fighting tooth and nail for your very existence. The majority do not survive the ambush attack.

Verbal communication nearly always precedes an attack upon the victim, who is quite often disarmed or shocked rigid by it. The time lapse between the disarming or scarifying verbal (which can be very short) and the attack itself is your time. During these seconds the victim may seize the moment, as it were, and be pre-emptive, effecting attack or escape, or elongate the verbal by replying to the aforementioned dialogue with aggressive counter-verbal, unbalancing the attacker's psyche. These seconds before battle are absolutely pivotal and must be managed quickly and without demur; remember, hesitancy begets defeat. This arena is that of the three second fighter.

When police talk about self-protection, the key is target hardening, that is, making yourself a hard target by means of placement and awareness of environment and the enemy. When I talk about the physical aspect of self-protection I am always working on the premise that, for whatever reason, a situation has gone beyond this and reached dire straits and the possibility of escape is no longer an option or that option has been lost.

As we have said, pre-fight management is vital if you want to survive intact. Who wins and who loses in most situations is usually determined by what happens pre-fight as opposed to in-fight. Most situations start at conversation range, this being talking or handshake distance. If this is mismanaged it degenerates rather quickly to vertical grappling range and then ground fighting—not a good place to be if you don't know the arena. While conversation distance is not the chosen range of the majority—most people feel safer at about four or five feet—it can be maintained so that it does not degenerate further into grappling range by 'putting a fence around your factory'.

If you had a factory that you wanted to protect from robbers the most sensible thing to do would be to place a fence around it to make it a hard target so that a potential robber has got to get past that fence before he can even think about attacking the factory. While the fence might not keep him out indefinitely it will make his job decidedly harder. Rather like a boxer who constantly flicks a jab into his opponent's face, even if that jab does not hurt his opponent it still keeps him at bay, and if his opponent wants to employ his knock out blow he first has to find a way past his opponent's jab. To the boxer, the jab is the fence around his factory.

In self-protection the fence around your factory is your lead hand, placed in that all-important space between you and your antagonist to maintain a safe gap. Like the factory fence, the lead hand will not keep an aggressor at bay forever—just long enough for you to initiate an escape or a pre-emptive attack—but it will place you in charge, even though your aggressor may not know it. Placed correctly the lead hand will not only maintain a safe gap but it will also disable the attacker's armory of right- and left-hand techniques, knee thrusts, head-butts, etc. Though he may not know it on a conscious level, he will instinctively realize that, until that fence has been removed or by-passed, his techniques have no clear way through.

Sensory Tentacle

The lead hand should be held in a non-aggressive way and should not touch the aggressor unless he makes a forward movement and tries to bridge the gap between you and him. It acts as a sensory guide to your aggressor's intentions; if he moves forward he will touch the fence and set your alarm bells ringing—this forward movement should be checked so as to maintain the safe range by using the palm of the lead hand on the aggressor's chest. Don't hold the touch as this may be seen by your assailant, on a conscious level, as a controlling movement (while of course it is a controlling action, it's better at this stage that the aggressor does not feel that you are in control). This will force him to knock your hand away or grab your wrist and possibly cause him to attack you prematurely, so as soon as you have checked him return the lead hand to its standby position.

One of the final subliminal precursors to an aggressor's attack is distance close down. If he tries to bridge the gap that you are maintaining it is usually because he is making his final preparations for assault, so if he does move forward and touch the fence you should, as well as checking range, be getting ready to make a pre-emptive attack or suffer the consequences should he break down the fence. In my opinion the maximum amount of times that a potential attacker should be allowed to touch the fence is twice – after that you've got big problems and will probably end up in a match fight situation or on the floor with a crowd around you, depending upon the caliber of fighter you are facing. Every time the attacker touches the fence the danger doubles.

The fence should look and feel *natural*; this will come with practice. If it doesn't and the attacker notices it on a conscious level he will try to knock it away and bridge the gap. Ideally the fence should be fluid, always moving, like you are using your hands to talk.

A professional may notice the fence no matter how well you disguise it and try using deceptive dialogue or body language to bring the fence down. Once down he will act. This often entails telling you that he does not want trouble, or that he just wants to talk; he may ask directions, the time, your name, anything to disarm you enough to lower the fence. An experienced fighter will offer to shake hands to get rid of the fence or try to close the gap by putting his arm around your shoulder in a pally kind of way. Don't have any of it – if there is the slightest chance of threat then don't let anyone touch you; a good fighter will only need one shot once the fence is down, so keep it up. If he still persists in coming forward and you don't feel ready to strike, or indeed are not even sure that a strike is called for, don't hesitate to back-up the check with a firm verbal fence: *Stay where you are!*

With the modern enemy the rule of thumb is, *if his lips are moving he's lying*, so don't believe a word that he says. If he still persists in coming forward then he has given you the 'go'. Having said all that, if the potential attacker has already made his intentions obvious by demanding your wallet or threatening you then there is nothing to contemplate: you should go the first time he touches the fence.

Range Finder

The fence also acts as a range finder. Many trained fighters misjudge the distance of their attacks in a real situation because the range is foreign to them. By touching the opponent with the lead hand before initiating your attack you can judge the exact distance, giving you a more accurate and solid shot.

Action Trigger

If and when you have decided to initiate an attack the lead hand also acts as a physical action trigger. You touch the opponent with the lead hand, finding the range, and bounce off the touch using it to trigger your attack. This should be coupled with the verbal brain engaging action trigger detailed earlier.

Multiple Attackers

The fence can also be used to maintain the range and even position of multiple attackers, but this is tantamount to fighting on more than one front. It is very difficult to maintain the range of more than one attacker and a speedy decision to attack or escape should always be sought.

The fence can be constructed in any way you choose as long as it blocks the gap and looks inoffensive. You can use a stop fence by placing the palm of the lead hand in front of the opponent, but this will bring the control to a conscious level and may catalyse alarm in the opponent. Where possible it is best to control him without him knowing it.

Once you have put up the fence and lined up the antagonist with your chosen technique (this should be done within the first seconds of any confrontation) and you are sure that an attack upon your person is imminent, utilize the response sequence previously detailed. If you have to attack, distract and engage your opponent's brain with your chosen trigger. Then, if no other option is open to you, make a pre-emptive strike from your pre-cocked, chambered position. Your engaging verbal distraction will thus veil your attack.

OTHER COMBAT CONSIDERATIONS

There are numerous conditions and considerations that positively or otherwise impact the outcome of a hand-to-hand encounter. Everyone knows this on some level, but it bears repeating with respect to training. Whenever you train, train to engage *under adverse conditions*, remembering that situations are rarely ideal, often occuring at a time and place *not* of your choosing. Real fights rarely happen at the gym or dojo, where you are already warmed up, optimally attired, and in the proper mindset. Nor is the contemporary sadist, thug, predator going to ask you to step outside behind the bar, give you time to remove your jacket, roll up your sleeves, draw your weapon, and assume a proper guard stance.

Practice in confined quarters, encumbered by how you're currently attire, weapon unavailable, and *not* in a ready stance. Many serious martial artists aleady train in the manner, but this is merely the start of training under adverse conditions. Start by experimenting with the four variables below as conditions that do not necessarily favor you—

Distance

Train against assailants who are "in your face" *and* constantly "just out of reach." Both situations can be extreme; and you may believe the "out of reach" condition is easier until you realize that he won't stop until you stop him! And what if you're with the wife and kids, and he—or they—are dogging you? Stopping him will require you to effectively *bridge the gap*.

Terrain

Work backwards: dojo/padded floor; wooden floor; garage floor; sidewalk; grass; dirt; sand; gravel. Don't just practice the combat you, *ahem*, specialize in—box, wrestle, play formal judo. Train in the pool or at the beach. See how fast you are *there*.

Terrain

Mobility

Again, many martial artists are already doing some of this, but perhaps not all of this: beging the engagement sitting deep in a chair; in a car; in a (simulated) theater[24], on your knees, *without* the option of rising; on a stairway.

---

24 Generally *less* mobility than in a car.

Physical Strength and Status

This is something most martial artists have done—do *more* of it! Off hand incapacitated; strong hand incapacitated; hands bound in front; hands bound in back; legs bound at knees, with a 12" space between them; legs bound at ankles, with a 12" space between them; legs firmly bound at ankles.

Impaired Strength and Status

Add other adverse conditions that you already do, or that exist in your day-to-day work or living environment. Consider environmental or architectural aspects, such fences, tunnels, elevators, crowds. Learn to access your *kakushi-buki*[25] in all situations. Learn to access other weapons as well, whether you normally carry them or not: pocket knife; telescoping baton; sidearm, etc. *Why*, you might wonder, *if you don't generally rely on such arms?* Because the training itself you make you a better and more resourceful fighter.

---

25 Hidden or disguised weapons

**Left to right, clockwise: *Yumio Nawa, Sho Kosugi, Takamatsu Toshitsugu,
Masaaki Hatsumi, Fujita Seiko*, and *Shoto Tanemura***

WHO IS A NINJA?

At this point, after having read through some of the philosophical, psychological, and physical concepts that are encompassed in *Shinobi-no-Michi*, both the disillusioned and the active practitioner will have a better sense of how their present activities align with the traditional principles of ninjutsu. But what of the novice who has yet to engage in the formal practice of ninjutsu under the banner of any of the many organizations that exist today? *Where do they stand at this point*?

For some readers, the term *ninja* will conjure up the image of my old friend, actor Sho Kusugi[26], wreaking his inimitable brand of *shinobi* vengeance on deserving evil-doers. Other readers, thinking themselves more knowledgeable, will associate the term *ninja* with grandmaster Masaaki Hatsumi[27], the iconic founder of the irrepressible Bujinkan organization. Yet, having interacted extensively with both men, I can say that both types of readers are decidedly *wrong*. This statement may possibly confuse some readers and outrage others. Mr. Kosugi, of course, acknowledges that he is an actor who portrayed ninja. Dr. Hatsumi, on the other hand, insists that he is, in his own words to me, "*honto ninja*" – the only *true* ninja.

---

26 **Sho Kosugi** has starred in many ninja action movies, none of which portray what ninjutsu actually is.
27 **Masaaki Hatsumi** has written many books about ninjutsu, few of which have anything to do with what the art actually is.

The Empty Cup and Open Mind

For the rare reader who lacks a frame of reference for what a shinobi should be, perhaps the best example is, ironically, the *fictitious Yukishiro Sanada*[28], author of an excellent book improbably titled, **Ninja Training Manual**. If you have read that book, you will know why.

The reader who is *not currently involved in the practice of Ninjutsu* will find it easier to keep an open mind than the so-called, "trained" Ninjutsu practitioner. And readers who *are* active in Ninjutsu will need to adopt a mental *kamae*, i.e., a posture or attitude, that is too often lacking in the pursuit of their art. It is a *kamae* that many are intellectually familiar with *but few are actually capable of assuming*. That *kamae* is **objectivity**. Reading through this monograph with a suspension of emotion and ego will allow you to approach its contents with the all-important "empty cup."

From personal experience, I recognize that this is not an easy task. Many have been the times when, in reading a new book, I have come across something that I consider to be a mistake or error on the author's part. Obsessing on that error or point of disagreement has deterred me from reading further, and led me to cast the book aside. In essence, I have allowed a *few points* of disagreement to lead me to *dismiss the entire book* as inaccurate or worthless—admittedly to my loss.

---

28 *Yukishiro Sanada* is a pseudonym for **Toshishiro Obata**, a well-known and well-rounded martial artist who is also an actor, writer, and was trained by, among others, Ninjutsu master Yumio Nawa.

Perhaps the book I disregarded contained something of greater value, but I was unwilling to read further because my cup was full of my own "opinions" or "expertise." Today, I try not to judge a book—or author—merely because the book or author contains a few points with which I disagree or know to be erroneous. Instead, *I continue reading with the expectation*, one often met, *that I will still find something beneficial and insightful* only a few pages away.

Some Tea for Your Cup

Returning to the original question of *Who is a ninja*, I find it naïve to believe—as some of my American Bujinkan friends *still* do—that ninja were spiritually-evolved underdogs who only became spies and assassins because they felt compelled to defend their families from the inequities they were subject to. *Why do I say this?* Because as an educator in my nine-to-five work life, I know that spiritual evolution comes from a combination of *education* and *introspection*. Historically, *the classical ninja lacked both!*

Having to till the soil, grow your food, raise your family, make your weapons, get around without a car, a bullet train, or even a horse, and train in the physical arts *if* you still had time, (and if you were not looking over your shoulder to check that Oda Nobunaga or his sons were planning to raze your *mura*[29] to the ground), you had little time or means left for a formal education, let alone time for introspection and spiritual evolution. Samurai operated on pre-established tenets, and ninja operated on legacy cunning. Neither was encouraged to

---

29 "Village", for those of you unfamiliar with the term.

think for themselves as that might lead to their not following orders[30].
That is often why both 1) tended to be superstitious, and 2) blindly
went through the motions of things they didn't actually understand—
such as *kuji-kiri*, or chanting spells, or killing on command! The
copious "ninja books" on the market today not only romanticize the
historical shinobi, but are actually contradicted by the documented
accounts recorded by a highly literate Japanese culture. It would prove
advantageous to shed the many false notions that have been
perpetuated in the writings of "ninja experts" and become receptive to
a better understanding of who the historical shinobi actually was.

---

30 Much like today's Ninpo followers, er ... I mean, *practitioners.*

There were very few common denominators shared by the diverse individuals who we too conveniently lump under the term *ninja*. Some were menial foot soldiers (like *ashi garu*), some were intelligence gatherers (*monomi*), others brilliant military strategists (*heihojin*), and still others immoral killers. What this means is that *we cannot make broad general statements about who ninja*, as a group, *were.*

- **Not everyone** who we classify as a ninja *dressed in black uniforms*; in fact, it is unlikely they even wore uniforms.

- **Not everyone** who we classify as a ninja *was multi-skilled in every art* we regard as a ninja art. Most were merely specialists in specific strategies and tactics.

- **Not everyone** who we classify as a ninja *was a feudal-age covert operative*. Those of higher rank were more akin to administrators and negotiators than shadow warriors.

- **Not everyone** who we classify as a ninja was a *skilled fighter or expert at hand-to-hand combat*. In fact, to have to fight meant that one had *failed* because, *by definition*, a ninja is compelled to be "invisible."

- **Not everyone** who we classify as a ninja was the *cultural or philosophical antithesis of the samurai*. In fact, the ninja and samurai often had similar backgrounds, practiced similar martial arts, and held similar cultural beliefs.

Moreover, shinobi did not have **dojo** as we understand the term, where they went to train after a hard day's work in the rice fields. They had no **structured curriculum**, like we have today, with a vast number of techniques that practitioners are required master to pass on their painstaking path to acquiring a coveted black belt. *There was no black belt!*

Instead, martial prowess in areas such as unarmed combat or sword handling was generally passed on in a father-to-son manner. For that reason, an particular shinobi's skill in a given martial area was limited by the skill of the person who taught him. *This is probably a major reason why shinobi were historically predisposed to rely on deceit, trickery*, and a reliance on what my old friend, Charles Daniel, calls "surprise self defense weapons." As Charles describe[31], *"Surprise self defense weapons include those weapons that the opponent learns about only too late."*

As a group, shinobi did not lead lives that were rigidly driven by their religious beliefs. This is largely a fabricated notion, first advanced by Toei Studios in their 1960s **Shinobi-no-Mono** films, and later "corroborated" by American writers in the 1980s—who had their obvious motives for *sanitizing* the image of the deadly art they were first starting to *sell*. You see, mainsteam Japan did *not* regard the shinobi as *noble*. That is why it was not until the last quarter of the 20th century that legitimate Ninjutsu practitioners—*Seiko Fujita,*

---

31 In his invaluable book, **Traditional Ninja Weapons**.

Yumio Nawa, Heishichiro Okuse, Jinichi Kawakami, etc—even admitted to being involved in the art.

u

I could go on, but the point should be obvious: there was no *one* shinobi archetype. What this should make clear is that, contrary to the claims of "ninja experts," historical shinobi varied immensely in their training, their skills, their motivations, and their existential beliefs. *How then, can modern ninja purport to be the arbiters of what is "legitimate" Ninjutsu and what is not.*

Bujinkan Students are Authentic Ninja, *or Are They?*

The *"quality of your Taijutsu"* or other fighting ability has little to do with being a ninja. UFC contenders have excellent fighting abilities, but that by itself does not qualify them as ninja. Lineage and/or possession of *rare ninja scrolls* has little to do with being a ninja. As already mentioned in Chapter 2, one of the first English language books that *accurately* described Ninjutsu to the western reader was **Zen Combat**, an overview of Eastern martial arts written by journalist Jay Gluck in 1962. Among the many concepts he discusses, Gluck informs us that his own Japanese wife's uncle was the inheritor of his family's ninja *densho*[32]. However, because they were in a dialect and written language system that was no longer in use, the densho's contents were unintelligible.

---

32 Written teachings.

By the way, here's what Mr. Gluck had to say about ... well, Gluck never specifically said *who*, but you can guess:

> *None of the many self-acclaimed modern ninja I have met have given the slightest indication that they possess any special powers, though they are popularly attributed with many. One famous ninja near Tokyo, featured in an article in a popular men's magazine, claims, as do many, to be "the last master of ninjutsu alive." But the only art he practices, outside of a cockeyed form of karate, is the use of dirty weapon – highly impractical to carry around and overspecialized to a point of being themselves highly vulnerable – of a coarseness and primitiveness that would make even a dead-end thug flinch.*

Yes; this was written in Japan around 1962, and you have guessed correctly. Dr. Hatsumi!

Historical experts are not necessarily shinobi, although in my opinion, *they are among the ones who often have the most potential for becoming one.* The "iconoclast" Antony Cummins, for example. Historians tend to be objective. Moreover, they don't "drink the Kool-Aid" that *true believers become intoxicated on.*

Heart of a Flower

Many Ninpo practitioners are quick to regurgitate the gibberish that past ninjutsu personages wrote, believing that such artistic and quasi-religious concepts encapsulate the meaning of the art. Almost any tome you pick up will contain quotes of this type, e.g.,

The heart of a warrior means a sincere heart. As **Kajo Chikusei** *teaches us, one must strive to be as gentle as a flower, and as straight— moreover, as straightforward—as bamboo.*
—Takamatsu Toshitsugu

Or another quote from a recent **Shihan Essence.com** poster:

> *There have been too many people pretending to understand things that they cannot possibly understand. And what is worse, they are passing themselves off as knowledgeable and are teaching others. This is a true shame.*
> —Soke Masaaki Hatsumi
> Bujinkan Budo Taijutsu ~~Ninjutsu~~

I personally feel that the second quote, from Dr. Hatsumi, is particularly *ironic*. While I concede that instructors have the right to express their personal sentiments concerning what their art means to them, *no one person can be regarded as the spokesperson for Ninjutsu* —an art that has spanned centuries and was practiced well, and sometimes not so well, by a variety of exponents. As the late Ronald Duncan, my own Ninjutsu instructor, often reminded us,

> *No one nation has a monopoly on Truth;*
> *no one country has a monopoly on the Sun.*

We can look at the more standardized—not to mention *venerated*—concept of **Bushido** and discover the same phenomenon. The seven virtues of Bushido were set down by Inazo Nitobe, but there is an overabundance of evidence to show that very few samurai followed each of its tenets.

Many modern-day ninjutsu practitioners fail to realize that codes of honor and behavior are generally written specifically *because the behaviors they espouse are typically absent in the people they are written for*. When I went to parochial school, we were surrounded by signs admonishing us not to talk in class, or eat before lunchtime, or have fights in the schoolyard. You don't have to have attended parochial school to understand why.

The point to be made here is that adherence to the virtues of Bushido was not necessarily how samurai comported themselves. It was merely an ideal that some *aspired* to; and the same is the case with the lofty, pseudo-moralistic writings that are often-cited to "describe" the pragmatic (not spititual) spies and mercenaries we today call by the modern name, ninja.

So, Then, Who is a Ninja Today?

Well, if you ask *nine different ninjutsu instructors*, wearing red belts with their names written *in kanji that they cannot read*, you'll probably get *eighteen different answers!* My own response, worth as much or as little as you want it to be, is this—

A ninja is a very careful man or woman. *Regardless of gender, a Ninja is a person who has spent due time considering how best to live his or her life safely and danger-free; or as danger-free as can be feasibly foreseen or anticipated.* **Foresight, preparation,** *and* **vigilance,** *then, are the key character attributes of the ninja.*

The antithesis of the Ninja was **not** *the Samurai. In fact, the Samurai himself possessed many Ninja-like qualities. The antithesis of the Ninja is the person who goes through life from day to day without due preparation or a well thought-out set of skills. When a threat or hazard* *manifests itself, the ninja antithesis is completely unprepared. Or he's prepared in only one way, perhaps with a strong punch or a sharp knife. He reacts instinctively but unthinkingly. Sometimes his reactions are appropriate; most often they are not—because their "trained reactions" are never broad in scope.*

*By thinking ahead, the ninja antithesis might have avoided the threat. If avoidance was impossible, by thinking ahead he may have been able to contend with it in a safe manner. He might have had a counter; or a cure; or some form of planned and practiced response. By thinking ahead he would have qualified as a careful man. By being **very** careful he would have been a Ninja.*

About the Author

In 1984, James Loriega founded the **New York Ninpokai**, a training facility which soon came to be regarded as *"the premier academy for the traditional shinobi arts in NYC."* Loriega began his formal martial arts training in 1967 with the late Grandmaster Ronald Duncan, the first non-Japanese to teach the shinobi arts in the United States—and the acknowledged *Father of American Ninjutsu.* Though he later trained with other ninjutsu masters, it was from Duncan-sensei that Loriega learned the myriad strategies, tactics, techniques, and disciplines of the ancient *shinobi.*

During the mid- to late-80s, Loriega also studied other Japanese martial arts, including *Aikijujutsu, Taijutsu, Jojutsu, and Hojojutsu.* Loriega began writing extensively around that same time, and from 1985 to 1995 served as Technical Consultant and Contributing Editor for **Ninja** magazine, an international publication dedicated exclusively to ninjutsu.

His overseas travels to teach ninjutsu also exposed Loriega to the western martial arts of Europe and the Mediterranean, and his subsequent training in those arts led to instructor ranks in other disciplines.

In January of 2002, Loriega was recognized as a master in western arts by the *International Masters-at-Arms Federation* (IMAF), based in Milan, Italy. The IMAF, now dissolved, was an organization of professional instructors of Historical and Classical edged weapons.

In February of 2018, he was recognized by the *Martial Arts University* as a *Martial Arts Icon*—an individual who is symbolic of an idea and leaves a memorable mark on the lives of those he teaches.

In April of 2018, he was recognized as a *Ninjutsu Scholar* and inducted into the *International Circle of Masters* (ICM).

Loriega holds instructor ranks in Ninjutsu, Jujutsu, and Aikijujutsu, as well as in a number of Western martial arts.

He has published over a dozen books on martial arts and martial culture, and his extensive writings have appeared in mainstream martial arts publications such as **Black Belt, Inside Kung-Fu, Ninja,** and **Tactical Knives**.

Inquiries for seminars or workshops may be sent to:

Ninpokai@aol.com

桂男

Bibliography

Adams, Andrew. **Ninja, *The Invisible Assassins***. Burbank, Ca: Ohara Publication. 1971

Collins, Patrick. **Living in Troubled Lands.** Boulder, CO: Paladin Press. 1981

Cummins, Antony. **Iga and Koka Ninja**: *Skills The Secret Shinobi Scrolls of Chikamatsu Shigenori*. Gloucestershire, UK: The History Press. 2013

Daniel, Charles. **Traditional Ninja Weapons** :Unique Publications

Draeger, Donn F. and Robert W. Smith. **Asian Fighting Arts**. Tokyo, New York, San Francisco: Kodansha International, Ltd. 1969

– **Ninjutsu, *The Art of Invisibility*.** Tokyo: Lotus Press. 1971

– **Classical Bujutsu.** New York: John Weatherhill, Inc. 1973

Gilbey, John. (Pseudonym for Robert W. Smith) **Secret Fighting Arts of the World**. Rutland, Vt. and Tokyo, Japan: Tuttle. 1963

Gluck, Jay. **Zen Combat**. New York: Ballantine Books. 1962

Gruzanski, Charles V. **Spike and Chain:** *Japanese Fighting Arts*. Rutland, Vt. and Tokyo, Japan: Tuttle.

Harrison, E. J. **The Fighting Spirit of Japan.**

Kotani, Ken. (Chiharu Kotani, trans.) **Japanese Intelligence in World War II**. Oxford, England: Osprey Publishing. 2009

Loriega, James. **Ninso:** *Ninjutsu's Art of Face Reading*. New York: Pay-Per-Cut Press. 2017

– **The Serpent and the Dove:** *The Shinobi Wisdom of Baltasar Gracián*. New York: Pay-Per- Cut Press. 2017

– **Ninjutsu and The Book of War**. New York: Lost Arts Publications. 2018

– **Ninjutsu and the Strategies of Wu Tzu**. New York: Lost Arts Publications. 2018

– **Shinobi-no-Michi:** *The Path of the Ninja*. New York: Lost Arts Publications. 2018

Luna, J.J. **How To Be Invisible.** New Yourk, NY: Thomas Dunne Books. 2012

Onoda, Hiroo. (Charles S. Terry, trans.) **No Surrender:** *My Thirty Year War*. Tokyo, New York & San Francisco: Kodansha International. 1974

Seiko, Fujita. **What Is Ninjutsu?** Eric Shahan, translator. CreateSpace Independent Publishing. 2017

– **The Eighteen Weapons of War**. Eric Shahan, translator. CreateSpace Independent Publishing. 2017

Simpson, WB. **Special Agent in the Pacific, World War II**. New York: Rivercross Publishing.1995

Sun Tzu. **The Art of War.** Lionel Giles, translator. London: Lozac. 1910

Webb, William. **No Surrender:** *Seven Japanese WWII Soldiers Who Refused to Surrender After the War*. www.AbsoluteCrime.com

Yagyu Munenori. **The Sword and the Mind**. Hiraoki Sato, translator. New York: The Overlook Press. 1986

www.ingramcontent.com/pod-product-compliance
Lightning Source LLC
Chambersburg PA
CBHW031248280526
45784CB00004B/1769